DID YOU KNOW?

For parents and children accustomed to long, time-consuming tests, it may seem impossible to truly gather sufficient placement information with just a few questions. But, the truth is that you can easily and effectively learn where to place your child academically in a subject with just twenty simple questions!

How is this possible? Well, keep in mind that most achievement tests are administered to large groups of students, and the results are processed through computers. Therefore, these tests require a minimum of three to five questions per topic in order to assess an average.

When a test is administered one on one and the parent walks through each question with their child, however, the assessment results are not strictly based on right or wrong answers. Instead, they are based on observation of thought processes, understanding of the question, and the ability to work through the question or problem. As a result, typically only one question, combined with interactive administration of the test, is required to adequately assess a child's level of understanding.

Well Planned Start includes both the administrator guide and step-by-step answer key in order for parents to confidently administer, observe, and evaluate the test-taking process to understand exactly where their children place.

A TOOL FOR PARENTS

As a mom of five, I began giving my kids achievement tests at an early age. After teaching them how to fill in the small circles and sharpen their number 2 pencils, the kids would walk into classrooms, doors would close, and testing would begin. Six weeks later, I would receive test reports which gave vague indications of how each child was doing compared to children across the nation. The broad descriptions of achievement in specific areas provided very little useful information to help me know how to strengthen my kids in the coming year.

Over the years, I sought an assessment option that would help me choose the best curriculum, cover information unknown to my child, and fill in any educational gaps. Unfortunately, none of the tests I found accomplished this goal. That needed to change!

Recognizing the need, I began working with the Well Planned Gal curriculum developer **Tiffany Orthman, M.Ed.** to develop a one-of-a-kind, easy-to-use assessment and placement test for parents and children to work through together.

Well Planned Start is unique as it guides you, the parent, to a better understanding of what your child knows, comprehends, and can process correctly. This educational evaluation tool offers a two-sided assessment. First, you will find a parent assessment, helping you discover what you know about your child. Second, a student placement test walks your child through a series of questions while you follow along with an administrator guide that helps you know how to process your child's answers and thinking processes.

Best of all, I've included helpful tips for each of the subjects and areas, as well as a checklist of milestones for this school year. Milestones work as a guide as you watch your child develop emotionally, physically, and educationally throughout the year.

As you proceed through this book and into your school year, remember these five key points:

- Relax! This is not a comparison or a judgment game. This is a tool to help you determine where your child is.

- Use the information to make improvements. Spend extra time or use a different approach where there are weaknesses. Offer more activities if you need to challenge your child. If you have not covered an area, now is the time!

- Try to set aside presuppositions as you begin the assessment. Remember, dislike for a subject does not indicate a weakness.

- These assessments are based on grasping concepts rather than parroting correct answers.

- Bible has been added as an additional component in these assessments. Keep in mind, though, that spiritual growth is not based on age. This is simply a resource to help you have an idea of where to look for and encourage growth.

Rebecca Farris
WELL PLANNED GAL

BOOK OVERVIEW

The Well Planned Start has been organized and arranged in order of sequence. Each section has an introduction with detailed information on how to assess your child, administer the placement test, and understand the milestones.

PARENT ASSESSMENT TESTS

The goal of this section is to become familiar with what your child knows. If your child has been attending school or hybrid homeschooling, this area will give you the opportunity to begin dialogues to understand the depth of understanding in each subject.

There are detailed instructions on how to use this assessment, as well as worksheets to journal your findings. At the end of this section, we give practical teaching tips to help you enhance each subject area.

STUDENT PLACEMENT TESTS

Unlike standardized testing, these placement tests allow parents to see first hand the specific areas children excel and need help in. By using the guide to administer the tests, you not only give instructions to your child, but you will also follow instructions that help you know what to watch for as the child works through the questions. This allows you to discover where the breakdown begins in the process.

PARENT TEACHING TIPS

After administering tests, you will find practical teaching tips and activity suggestions for every concept covered in the placement test. Use these suggested activities to strengthen low-scoring areas, keep your child challenged, fill in gaps, and more!

7TH GRADE MILESTONES

Complete with a checklist of milestones, Well Planned Start provides a year-long guide on what to expect from your child physically, emotionally, and academically. Beyond what they should achieve, we've included what they may achieve, including even advanced achievements. An additional checklist is included in each area to let you know how to help your child along the way.

TESTING OBSTACLES

If your child has never taken a test before or has trouble when testing, the Well Planned Start assessments offer a great introduction to testing and are relaxed enough to put any child at ease.

The assessments are not timed, and there are no little circles on separate sheets of paper that children have to navigate. Instead, parents are encouraged to engage children, review instructions, or stop for a break when needed.

In the comfort of your home and with the assurance of a parent administering the assessment, children working through Well Planned Start are able to relax, comprehend, access the information, and enjoy the experience.

Well Planned Start ensures an accurate and enjoyable assessment and placement for children and parents.

#1 START HERE

Begin with the Parent Assessment

PARENT ASSESSMENT

The following pages contain the parent assessment tests for math, language arts, history & geography, science, and Bible. Use this section to begin understanding what your child should know and comprehend. Here are a few tips as you proceed through the questions ahead:

- If you are unsure about the questions and answers, do a quick Internet search.

- If you are unsure whether a topic has been or will be covered, do a little digging. Speak to a representative at your child's previous school or take a quick look through your past or current homeschool curriculum.

- Engage your child in a discussion to see how deep his or her knowledge is. Remembering the significance of an event is more important than knowing a date for a test.

- Try to figure things out together. This is a team effort.

- Lack of information does not necessarily indicate a gap. For example, if you have not covered early American history yet but are sure your child would understand it, give your child credit for abilities.

- Watch your child's general attitude toward learning. If there is a lot of negativity, plan to take a step back to regain a love of learning.

- As you process through this assessment with your child, go with your gut instinct. If you feel your child is good at something, say so. If you feel he or she is struggling, say so.

- Think back to all the times you observed your child doing school work, playing, or having conversations. Do you feel that he or she understands the concepts?

- If you don't feel confident in your knowledge, ask for help from family and friends.

- Ask classmates, former teachers, or other homeschool moms what their observations of your child are.

- Be sure that you administer the entire assessment. If your assessment and your child's performance do not match up, investigate possible causes such as test anxiety or lack of information.

BEYOND ACADEMICS

Well Planned Start offers a great baseline for assessing grade placement and academic, emotional, and physical progress. But, be sure to remember your child's need to explore interests as well.

During 7th grade, you will see a narrowing of your child's interests from the wide exploration of the early elementary years as specific hobbies and activities become more appealing. Your child may progress to a more experienced level in skills begun in younger years, or this may be the year that groundwork is laid for interests that will develop further in high school.

Because academics begin to take more time during these middle school years, be proactive about preserving two to three opportunities a week specifically for pursuit and development of interests.

THE COORDINATE PLANE

	YES	NO
Can your child plot points on a coordinate plane?	○	○
Is your child able to identify the coordinates of a point on a plane?	○	○
Can your child calculate the distance between two points on the X axis?	○	○
Is your child able to calculate the distance between two points on the Y axis?	○	○

PROPORTIONS AND GEOMETRIC PROPORTIONS

	YES	NO
Is your student able to recognize proportions on tables and graphs?	○	○
Can your student use proportion to complete a table or graph?	○	○
Is your child able to solve problems involving percentages?	○	○
Can our child calculate the area of a figure when one of its dimensions changes?	○	○

GEOMETRY

	YES	NO
Can your child use formulae to find the areas and perimeters of plane figures?	○	○
Is your child able to construct symmetrical plane figures?	○	○
Can your child find the volume of a pyramid?	○	○
Is your student able to identify vertical, congruent, complementary, supplementary, adjacent, corresponding, alternate interior, and alternate exterior angles?	○	○

ALGEBRA AND NUMBER LINE

	YES	NO
Can your child solve an equation for one variable?	○	○
Does your child know the proper order of operations and the grouping symbols?	○	○
Can your child add and subtract signed decimal problems?	○	○
Is your child able to compare integers, signed decimals, and fractions?	○	○

PROBABILITY AND STATISTICS

	YES	NO
Can your child give the probability of an event happening?	○	○
Can your child create a circle graph?	○	○
Can your child create a bar graph?	○	○
Can your child find the mean, median, range, and mode of a set of numbers?	○	○

Math

SYMMETRICAL PLANE FIGURES

A coordinate plane is formed by a horizontal number line, called the x-axis, and a vertical number line, called the y-axis. The two axes intersect at a point called the origin.

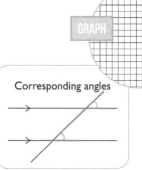

GRAPH

Corresponding angles

5th - 8th grade

BEGINNING TO UNDERSTAND

MATH

What was a subject full of fact memorization in the early years becomes much more practical in this stage of learning. Even children who have disliked math can grow to enjoy it as they see how ratios, fractions, and geometry apply to real life.

Encourage your child to help alter recipes or figure sales tax on a shopping trip to see math in real-life action!

PARENT ASSESSMENT

A research essay presents a student's own interpretation, evaluation, or argument on a given topic.

ROOTS

acer, acid, acri	bitter, sour, sharp
acu	sharp
ag, agi, ig, act	do, move, go
ali, allo, alter	other
alt(us)	high, deep
am, amor	love, liking
Anni, annu, enni	year
anthrop	man
anti(co)	old
arch	chief, first, rule

5th - 8th grade

BEGINNING TO UNDERSTAND LANGUAGE ARTS

As with math, components of grammar should solidify during these middle school years as your child begins to implement all of those isolated concepts learned in the early years.

This is the perfect time to work on writing skills and show the reason for learning about punctuation and parts of speech. Make it fun by creating silly stories and poems!

WRITING AND RESEARCH   YES   NO

Is your child able to write book reports, summaries, descriptive essays, stories, and poems?   ○   ○

Can your child write descriptive, narrative, persuasive, and compare and contrast essays?   ○   ○

Is your child able to write a good research essay?   ○   ○

Can your child write a piece completely independently?   ○   ○

SPEAKING AND LISTENING   YES   NO

Is your child able to have a conversation with adults?   ○   ○

Does your child enjoy group activities?   ○   ○

Can your child give a short speech to a group?   ○   ○

Does your child use standard English when speaking?   ○   ○

SPELLING AND VOCABULARY   YES   NO

Is your child able to build words from Latin and Greek roots?   ○   ○

Is your child familiar with the thesaurus?   ○   ○

Does your child enjoy using big words while speaking and writing?   ○   ○

Can your child spell commonly misspelled words?   ○   ○

GRAMMAR AND USAGE   YES   NO

Does your child understand prepositional phrases?   ○   ○

Can your child use correct subject-verb agreement with compound subjects?   ○   ○

Is your child familiar with direct objects, indirect objects, predicate nouns, and predicate adjectives?   ○   ○

Can your student identify participles, participial phrases, gerunds, gerund phrases, infinitives, and infinitive phrases?   ○   ○

LITERATURE   YES   NO

Is your child familiar with sonnets, lyrics, limericks, and haiku?   ○   ○

Can your child explain point of view, internal conflict, and external conflict?   ○   ○

Does your child know what a soliloquy and an aside are?   ○   ○

Can your child define irony, flashback, and foreshadowing?   ○   ○

WORLD HISTORY

	YES	NO
Can your child describe imperialism?	◯	◯
A policy of extending a country's power and influence through diplomacy or military force.		
Does your child know what caused World War I?	◯	◯
Is your child familiar with the Russian Revolution?	◯	◯
Can your child describe totalitarianism?	◯	◯
A system of government that is dictatorial and requires complete subservience to the state.		

WORLD GEOGRAPHY

	YES	NO
Is your child able to identify the physical features of Europe?	◯	◯
Can your child locate countries of Europe on a map?	◯	◯
Does your child know the capitals of European countries?	◯	◯
Is your child able to name the languages of Europe?	◯	◯

UNITED STATES HISTORY

	YES	NO
Does your child know about the Spanish-American War?	◯	◯
Is your child able to describe the Roaring Twenties?	◯	◯
Can your child tell you how the Great Depression started?	◯	◯
Does your child know about America's involvement in World War II?	◯	◯

UNITED STATES GEOGRAPHY

	YES	NO
Can your child identify the physical features of the United States?	◯	◯
Can your child describe the population distribution of the United States?	◯	◯
Can your child name regions of the United States and their characteristics?	◯	◯
Can your student locate the states and capitals?	◯	◯

CULTURE

	YES	NO
Is your child familiar with the art and music of the Harlem Renaissance?	◯	◯
Does your student understand how the stock market works?	◯	◯
Does your student take an interest in ethnic food?	◯	◯
Is your child familiar with art from around the world?	◯	◯

History
& Geography

The Spanish - American War was a conflict fought between Spain and the United States in 1898.

5th - 8th grade
BEGINNING TO UNDERSTAND
HISTORY & GEOGRAPHY

This stage stands as a strong bridge between the fun, general learning of the early years and the more targeted, reason-centered focus of high school.

This is a great time to utilize timelines and maps to show how various events in history intersect, laying the groundwork for the more idealogical lessons of the high school years.

Water Fire Wind Earth

💡 Mitosis is a method of cell division in which a cell divides and produces identical copies of itself.

5th - 8th grade
BEGINNING TO UNDERSTAND
SCIENCE

Middle school offers the perfect opportunity to "get serious" about science. But, that doesn't mean it stops being fun!

Use these years to meld the hands-on exploration of early learning with some definite book facts. But, keep it hands on with fun, engaging experiments, models, and activities. Doing science is still the best way to learn.

ATOMIC STRUCTURE

	YES	NO
Does your child know about the four Elements the Greeks taught?	○	○
Is your child familiar with alchemy?	○	○
Can your child use the periodic table?	○	○
Does your child know the parts of the atom?	○	○

CHEMICAL BONDS AND REACTIONS

	YES	NO
Is your child familiar with how atoms give away, take on, or share electrons?	○	○
Can your child explain chemical bonds?	○	○
Does your child know how reactions are expressed in equations?	○	○
Is your child able to tell you what a catalyst is?	○	○

A catalyst is a substance that speeds up a chemical reaction, but is not consumed by the reaction.

CELL DIVISION

	YES	NO
Can your child tell you what mitosis is?	○	○
Does your child understand meiosis?	○	○
Is your child familiar with haploid cells?	○	○
Can your child tell you what a diploid cell is?	○	○

GENETICS

	YES	NO
Does your child know what a mutation is?	○	○
Is your child familiar with well-known genetic researchers?	○	○
Can your child explain how DNA makes new DNA?	○	○
Does your child know what a chromosome is?	○	○

WEATHER

	YES	NO
Is your child familiar with the difference between weather and climate?	○	○
Can your child define the Coriolis effect?	○	○
Does your child know how fronts form?	○	○
Is your child able to describe the different types of storms?	○	○

Storms include thunderstorm, tornado, typhoon, and hurricane.

BIBLE STORIES

	YES	NO
Is your child familiar with the Old Testament prophets?	○	○
Does your child know the story of Joseph?	○	○
Can your child name some events from Jesus' ministry?	○	○
Does your child know the story of Esther?	○	○

BIBLE REFERENCE TOOLS

	YES	NO
Does your child know how to use a Bible dictionary?	○	○
Does your child know how to use the concordance in a Bible?	○	○
Can your child use the maps at the back of a Bible?	○	○
Can your child find a passage without turning to the Table of Contents?	○	○

BIBLE PASSAGES

	YES	NO
Is your child familiar with Psalm 1? *Blessed is the one who does not walk in step with the wicked...*	○	○
Is your child familiar with Ephesians 4:29? *Do not let any unwholesome talk come out of your mouths...*	○	○
Is your child familiar with the Romans Road?	○	○
Is your child familiar with John 1:7-10? *He came as a witness to testify concerning that light, so that through him all might believe...*	○	○

THEOLOGY

	YES	NO
Does your child understand atonement?	○	○
Does your child understand repentance?	○	○
Does your child know what a covenant is?	○	○
Does your child understand redemption?	○	○

CHURCH HISTORY & MISSIONS

	YES	NO
Does your child know who George Müller was?	○	○
Is your child familiar with George Whitefield?	○	○
Does your child know who William Carey was?	○	○
Is your child familiar with Amy Carmichael?	○	○

PROPHETS
Deborah
Samuel
Nathan
Elijah
Elisha
Huldah

Amy Carmichael: Missionary to India; founder of the Dohnavur Fellowship, a society devoted to saving neglected and ill-treated children

ATONEMENT
The reconciliation of God and mankind through the death of Jesus.

5th - 8th grade

BEGINNING TO UNDERSTAND

BIBLE

During these years, fun Bible stories give way to deeper concepts that will form the foundation for your child to hash out what he believes as he grows older.

Begin to introduce non-narrative portions of Scripture while also learning about the authors of each book of the Bible, how the Bible was compiled, and the history of the English translation.

MATH

Total Score

Score	Section
	The Coordinate Plane
	Proportions & Geometric Proportions
	Geometry
	Algebra & Number Line
	Probability & Statistics

Grade Placement

LANGUAGE ARTS

Total Score

Score	Section
	Writing & Research
	Speaking & Listening
	Spelling & Vocabulary
	Grammar & Usage
	Literature

Grade Placement

HISTORY & GEOGRAPHY

Total Score

Score	Section
	World History
	World Geography
	United States History
	United States Geography
	Culture

Grade Placement

SCIENCE

Total Score

Score	Section
	Atomic Structure
	Chemical Bonds & Reactions
	Cell Division
	Genetics
	Weather

Grade Placement

BIBLE

Total Score

Score	Section
	Bible Stories
	Bible Reference Tools
	Bible Passages
	Theology
	Church History & Missions

Grade Placement

PARENT ASSESSMENT SCORING

The Well Planned Start was designed to assess a grade level *per subject.* Use the key below to *determine the grade level for each subject.*

1. Count the number of questions you answered yes to in each section. Write the number in the score box to the left of the section.

2. Add the section scores together and place the total in the **Total Score** box.

3. Using the key below, determine the grade assessment for *each subject.*

SUBJECT TEST KEY

- Total Score = 20: Administer the 8th grade test for this subject. Your child may be ready for 9th grade.
- Total Score = 15-19: Your child is ready for the 8th grade.
- Total Score = 10-14: Base your decision on the following **section scores.**
  - Score 2 or less in 1-2 sections: Your child is ready for the 8th grade in this subject, but you can expect to give extra help throughout the year.
  - Score 2 or less in 3-5 sections: Your child should begin this subject at a 7th grade level.
- All sections = 0-9: Administer the 6th grade test for this subject. Your child needs additional evaluation.

BIBLE EXCEPTION

Because the development of spiritual growth is not confined to a grade level, the Bible tests for Well Planned Start were designed to cover a range through the following stages of education:

- Starting Out - Preschool - 1st Grade
- Getting Excited: 2nd - 4th Grade
- Beginning to Understand: 5th - 8th Grade
- Learning to Reason: 9th - 12th Grade

When scoring Bible and determining placement, it is recommended to use your discretion in deciding if additional testing is needed or more time studying the topics covered.

WHAT NEXT?

The parent assessment is a guide to what key information your child should know by the end of the 7th grade. Once you have finished taking the assessment and scoring the results, you can proceed to give the student placement assessment to confirm your results.

PARENT ASSESSMENT NOTES

Use this area to take notes about specific topics, subjects, and processes you feel your child will need help with. After your child has taken the placement test, compare your notes and the scores from the parent assessment to determine subject grades, overall grade level, and plan of action for the coming school year.

DETERMINING A
GRADE LEVEL

Assessment results can indicate grade levels below, at or above 7th grade. If you homeschool, you can purchase grade specific curriculum for each subject. However, if you are looking for a means to determine an overall grade level, use the suggestions below in deciding.

- If your child scores above or below a 7th grade level in math or language arts, you can easily incorporate materials from the assessed grade level. Your child should school in the 8th grade.

- If you child scores below a 7th grade level in three or more subjects (math, history, science, and language arts), we recommend repeating the 7th grade.

- If your child scores above a 7th grade level in three or more subjects (math, history, science, and language arts), we recommend testing with the 8th grade test for advanced placement.

- If your child scores ahead and behind in 2 or more subjects (math, history, science, and language arts), your child should school in the 8th grade.

- Reevaluate every year to be sure that your child is still at the correct grade.

#2 PROCEED

Proceed with Student Placement

The following pages contain the student placement tests for math, language arts, history and geography, science, and Bible. Along with the instructions on the test, there is also a section beginning on page 39 to reference as you watch your child work through the questions and answers. Utilizing this student placement test administrator guide will allow you to recognize the areas of struggle for your child and the point where problem solving breaks down.

The assessments ahead are a tool for you to use to better understand your child's academic needs. Here are a few more tips to use when administering these evaluations:

- Choose a calm day and a quiet space for assessment.

- Make sure your child is fresh and feeling well. Do not administer the assessments after three hours of calculus.

- Choose a time that is calm and fresh for you as well, as you will be working through the assessment with your child. It is important to minimize distractions for both you and your child during this time.

- Unless you have a child who enjoys tests and challenges, present these assessments as a new kind of activity or worksheet. If you say "test," they may lock up.

- Each assessment is printed on perforated pages. Simply remove each page and give it to the child to work on.

- Make sure your child understands the directions well.

- If the instructions are written in terms your child does not understand, feel free to change the wording.

- Take your time! These are not timed assessments. You are looking for correct thinking, not speed.

- As you process through this assessment with your child, go with your gut instinct. If you feel your child is good at something, say so. If you feel he or she is struggling, say so.

- Lack of information does not necessarily indicate a gap. For example, if you have not covered early American history yet but are sure your child would understand it, give your child credit for abilities.

- Look for creative thought processes. If you think an answer is weird, ask your child to explain how he or she arrived at it. If the logic behind the answer makes sense, give your child some credit.

- For concrete questions like math or science, watch for correct processes. Your child may be solving everything correctly and just writing down a wrong number or making a mistake in computation. If you are unsure, provide a new, similar problem for your child to work, or ask him to take another look. Having your child show his work will help.

- If you feel that there is a significant gap or that your child has not "gotten" the information after repeated exposure, please seek a professional evaluation for underlying issues. Whether you assign a label or not, understanding your child will make you a better teacher.

REMEMBER! ADMINISTRATOR GUIDE IS LOCATED BEHIND THE STUDENT TEST.

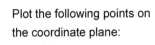

1. Plot the following points on the coordinate plane:

a. -1,2

b. 1,-2

c. 2,0

d. -1,-2

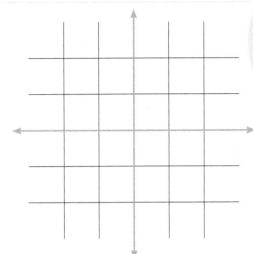

2. Identify the coordinates of the plots on the following plane:

1. _____

2. _____

3. _____

4. _____

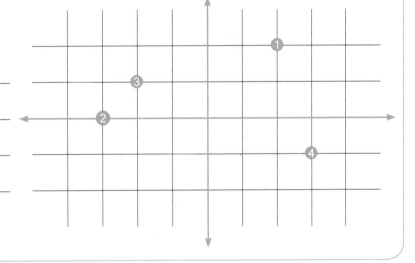

3. Using the above graph, what is the difference between point 1 and point 3 on the X axis?

4. Using the above graph, what is the difference between point 1 and point 4 on the Y axis?

Math

5. Fill in the missing proportions in the table below.

number of cupcakes	1	2		4	5	6		8
tablespoons of icing	4		12			24		

6. Use the proportions above to fill in missing information.

Graph with y-axis labeled "tablespoons of icing" (0 to 35) and x-axis labeled "number of cupcakes" (0 to 10). Points plotted at approximately (1, 4), (2.5, 16), (6, 24), (7.5, 32).

7. Look at the dimensions of the rectangle. Select the rectangle that is 33% smaller.

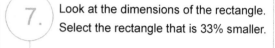

12 in
48 in

1. 6 in
    24 in

2. 4 in   16 in

3. 9 in
    36 in

Answer: _____

8. Look at triangle. What would be the area if the base were increased by 1?

Answer: _____

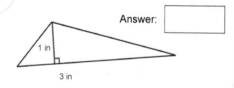

1 in

3 in

9. If a square has a perimeter of 12 ft, what is its area in sq. in.?

USE A SEPARATE SHEET OF PAPER TO WORK YOUR MATH PROBLEMS

10. Construct a symmetrical triangle with a base of 2 inches.

11. Find the volume of a pyramid:

base length: 3m

base width: 3m

pyramid height: 4m

12. Label the following angles as vertical, congruent, complementary, supplementary, adjacent, corresponding, alternate interior, and alternate exterior angles?

A.

B.

C.

D.

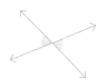

E.

F.

G.

H.

13. Solve to find x:

$$5x = \frac{25}{\times 5}$$

x =

14. Solve:

8 +[7 + (18 + 2)] - 6

15. Solve:

4 + (-7)

Math

16. Determine the largest number:

a.   -69 or -84 ☐

b.   -1.2 or 1.2 ☐

c.   1/6 or 1/2 ☐

17. If a box contains 4 oranges, 5 apples, and 6 nectarines, what are the chances that one will pick out an apple?

18. Create a circle graph showing the following:

2 students have blue eyes
4 have green eyes
11 have hazel eyes
9 have brown eyes

19. Find the mean, median, range, and mode of the following: 12, 12, 20, 16.

20. Create a bar graph for the following information:

Average Kilowatt Usage

California - 560
Montana - 850
Ohio - 910
Washington - 1,000
Colorado - 680

1. Match the type of writing with its description.

☐ book report   ☐ story

☐ summary   ☐ poem

☐ descriptive essay

a. a paper that describes a thing, event, process, or person

b. a piece of writing that partakes of the nature of both speech and song that is nearly always rhythmical, usually metaphorical, and often exhibits such formal elements as meter, rhyme, and stanzaic structure

c. an account of imaginary or real people and events told for entertainment

d. a way to show how well you understood a book and to tell what you think about it

e. a brief statement or account of the main points of something

2. Circle the things that you would include in a research essay.

introduction

title

signature

salutation

conclusion

closing

bibliography

3. Match the type of essay with its definition.

☐ descriptive   ☐ persuasive

☐ narrative   ☐ compare and contrast

a. a format in which the author tells, or narrates, a story

b. a paper that describes a thing, event, process, or person

c. multi-paragraph compositions that explain ways in which two subjects are similar or different

d. utilizes logic and reason to show that one idea is more legitimate than another idea

4. Explain how you tackle your writing assignments.

Language Arts

5. Select your feelings about conversing with adults

6. Share your feelings about group activities

7. Have you ever given a speech to a group?

8. Circle the standard English phrases.

raining cats and dogs	raining heavily
am not	ain't
in trouble	in the dog house
bite your tongue	please be quiet
stubborn as a mule	obstinate

9. Match the Latin or Greek root meanings

_____ambi
_____biblio
_____carnis
_____dent
_____eu

a. tooth
b. good, well
c. around, both
d. flesh
e. book

10. What would you find in a thesaurus:

a. synonyms
b. definitions
c. parts of speech

11. Match the word with its meaning.

☐ abate   ☐ docile

☐ beseech   ☐ exuberant

☐ canny

1. ready to accept control or instruction; submissive
2. having or showing shrewdness and good judgment, especially in money or business matters
3. led with or characterized by a lively energy and excitement
4. become less intense or widespread
5. ask someone urgently and fervently to do something; implore; entreat

Language Arts

12. Circle the misspelled word in each pair.

achievement	acheivement
dispise	despise
muscular	musculer
scholar	scholer
occassionally	occasionally

13. Underline the prepositional phrases in the following sentences:

When will we go to the store?

Did you take the meat out of the freezer?

A lot of people think sushi is good.

14. Select the correct verbs for the compound subjects.

Compound Subjects	Verbs	
She and I	was	were
Jake and he	are	is
Either they or I	am	are
Neither I nor he	am	is

15. Match each term with its definition.

☐ direct object

☐ indirect object

☐ predicate noun

☐ predicate adjective

1. a word or group of words that follows a linking verb or verb phrase and describes the noun

2. single noun or a noun phrase that renames the subject of a sentence and follows a form of the verb "to be" or another linking verb

3. a noun phrase denoting a person or thing that is the recipient of the action of a transitive verb

4. a noun phrase referring to someone or something that is affected by the action of a transitive verb, but is not the primary object

16. Match the grammatical terms with their definitions or examples.

☐ participle   ☐ gerund phrase

☐ participle phrase   ☐ infinitive

☐ gerund   ☐ infinitive phrase

1. eating ice cream

2. a form that is derived from a verb but that functions as a noun, in English ending in -ing

3. a word formed from a verb and used as an adjective

4. to smash a spider

5. the horse trotting up to the fence

6. the basic form of a verb, without an inflection binding it to a particular subject or tense

21

Language Arts

17. Match the type of poetry with the description

☐ sonnet ☐ lyric ☐ limerick ☐ haiku

1. a humorous verse of three long and two short lines rhyming in the aabba pattern, popularized by Edward Lear

2. a poem of fourteen lines using any of a number of formal rhyme schemes, in English typically having ten syllables per line

3. a Japanese poem of seventeen syllables, in three lines of five, seven, and five, traditionally evoking images of the natural world

4. have a musical rhythm, and their topics often explore romantic feelings or other strong emotions

18. A soliloquy is ☐

a. point in the play during which the tragic hero experiences a kind of self-understanding

b. a purgation of emotions

c. an act of speaking one's thoughts aloud when by oneself or regardless of any hearers, especially by a character in a play

19. Match the literary term with the definition

☐ point of view

☐ internal conflict

☐ external conflict

1. struggle between a literary or dramatic character and an outside force such as nature or another character, which drives the dramatic action of the plot

2. the narrator's position in relation to the story being told

3. psychological struggle within the mind of a literary or dramatic character, the resolution of which creates the plot's suspense

20. Match the literary term with the definition

☐ irony

☐ flashback

☐ foreshadowing

a. a warning or indication of a future event

b. a scene set in a time earlier than the main story

c. the full significance of a character's words or actions are clear to the audience or reader although unknown to the character

History
& Geography

Match the ideas and events that caused World War II with their descriptions.

1.

[ ] Nazi Party

[ ] Appeasement

[ ] Fascism

[ ] Japanese Expansion

[ ] Treaty of Versailles

1. Japan's practice or policy of territorial or economic expansion

2. the action of pacifying or placating someone by giving in to their demands

3. an authoritarian and nationalistic right-wing system of government and social organization

4. the political principles of the National Socialist German Workers' Party

5. a document signed between Germany and the Allied Powers following World War I that officially ended that war

2. Imperialism is [ ]

a. a political and economic theory of social organization that advocates that the means of production, distribution, and exchange should be owned or regulated by the community as a whole

b. a policy of extending a country's power and influence through diplomacy or military force

c. an authoritarian and nationalistic right-wing system of government and social organization

3. Totalitarianism is [ ]

a. constitutional government

b. a system of government by the whole population or all the eligible members of a state, typically through elected representatives

c. a system of government that is centralized and dictatorial and requires complete subservience to the state

4. Match the people and ideas of the Russian Revolution with the descriptions.

[ ] Rasputin

[ ] Russian Social - Democrat Labor Party

[ ] Communist Party

[ ] Nicholas II

[ ] Vladimir Lenin

a. a revolutionary socialist political party formed in 1898 in Minsk to unite the various revolutionary organizations of the Russian Empire into one party

b. Siberian peasant monk who was very influential at the court of Czar Nicholas II and Czarina Alexandra

c. reign was marked by defeat in the Russo-Japanese War, the 1905 Revolution, the influence of Rasputin, involvement in World War I, and governmental incompetence

d. Russian founder of the Bolsheviks and leader of the Russian Revolution and first head of the USSR

e. a political party that advocates the application of the social and economic principles of communism through state policy

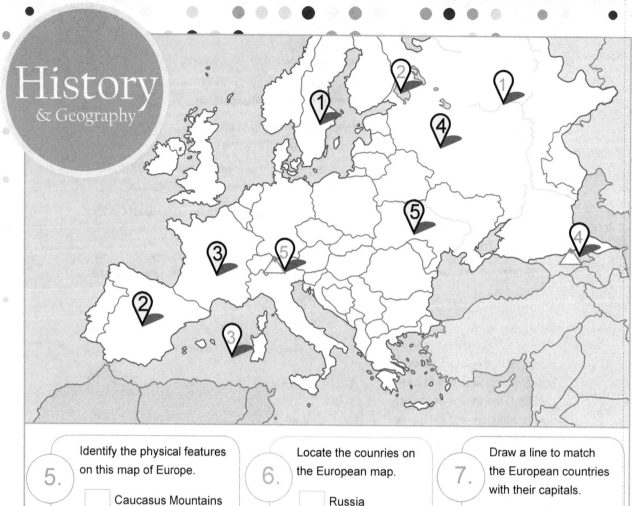

5. Identify the physical features on this map of Europe.

☐ Caucasus Mountains

☐ Volga River

☐ The Alps

☐ Lake Ladoga

☐ Mediterranean Sea

6. Locate the counries on the European map.

☐ Russia

☐ Ukraine

☐ France

☐ Spain

☐ Sweden

7. Draw a line to match the European countries with their capitals.

Germany	Warsaw
Turkey	Istanbul
UK	Berlin
Italy	London
Poland	Rome

8. Match the language with the European country.

PARIS
ROME
LONDON

1. French

2. Polish

3. English

4. German

5. Italian

_____ Germany

_____ Italy

_____ UK

_____ France

_____ Poland

9. Match the events and people of the Spanish American war.

☐ Battle of Santiago

☐ Emilio Auginaldo

☐ William McKinley

☐ Treaty of Paris

☐ *USS Maine*

1. A second-class battleship commissioned in 1895 that was part of the new U.S. Navy fleet of steel ships; it exploded in Havana Harbor in 1898 and precipitated U.S. entry into the Spanish-American War

2. An American politician and lawyer who served as the 25th President of the United States from March 4, 1897, until his assassination in September 1901, six months into his second term

3. A naval battle that occurred on July 3, 1898, in which the United States Navy decisively defeated Spanish forces, sealing American victory in the Spanish–American War and achieving nominal independence for Cuba from Spanish rule

4. An agreement made in 1898 that involved Spain relinquishing nearly all of the remaining Spanish Empire, especially Cuba, and ceding Puerto Rico, Guam, and the Philippines to the United States

5. A Filipino general who played an important role in the Philippine Revolution against Spain and later led Filipino insurgent soldiers against American forces

10. Match the ideas, events, and people of the Roaring Twenties.

☐ Yankee Stadium

☐ Kellogg–Briand Pact   ☐ Palmer Raids

☐ Warren G. Harding   ☐ Ernest Hemingway

1. A series of raids conducted by the United States Department of Justice to capture, arrest and deport suspected radical leftists, especially anarchists, from the United States

2. A political leader of the late nineteenth and early twentieth centuries, who served as president from 1921 to 1923

3. A stadium located in the Bronx, a borough of New York City; serves as the home ballpark for the New York Yankees of Major League Baseball

4. An American novelist, short story writer, and journalist

5. A treaty renouncing war as an instrument of national policy and urging peaceful means for the settlement of international disputes, originally signed in 1928 by 15 nations, later joined by 49 others

11. Circle the events that led to the Great Depression.

Spanish American War	Stamp Act
Construction boom ends	World War II
Stock market crashes	Obamacare
Economic excess	Bank panics

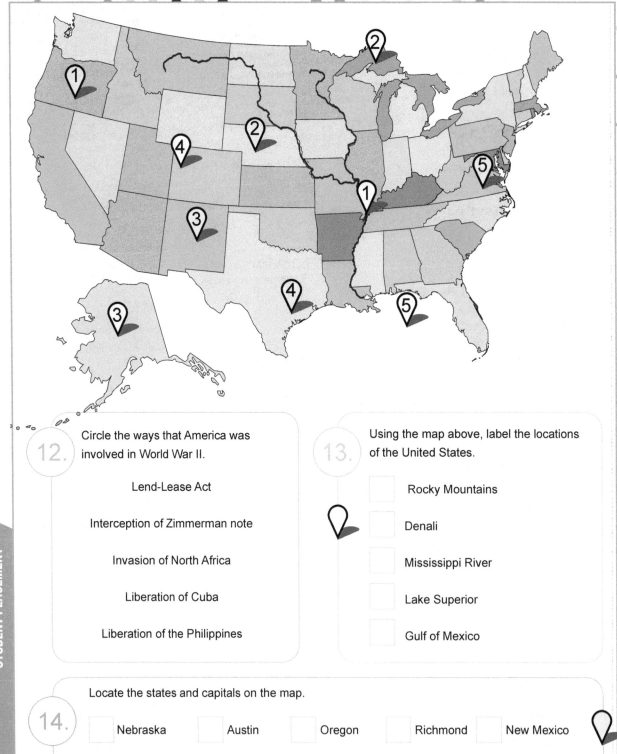

12. Circle the ways that America was involved in World War II.

Lend-Lease Act

Interception of Zimmerman note

Invasion of North Africa

Liberation of Cuba

Liberation of the Philippines

13. Using the map above, label the locations of the United States.

☐ Rocky Mountains

☐ Denali

☐ Mississippi River

☐ Lake Superior

☐ Gulf of Mexico

14. Locate the states and capitals on the map.

☐ Nebraska ☐ Austin ☐ Oregon ☐ Richmond ☐ New Mexico

15. Put the U.S. cities in order by population starting with the most populous.

☐ Chicago

☐ Philadelphia

☐ Houston

☐ Los Angeles

☐ New York

16. Match the regions of the United States with their characteristics.

☐ Sun Belt

☐ West Coast

☐ Mason-Dixon Line

1. known for surfing, coffee, and sunny weather

2. boundary between Maryland and Pennsylvania

3. noted for resort areas and for the movement of businesses and population into these states from the colder northern states

17.

Match the artists and musicians of the Harlem Renaissance

☐ Billie Holiday

☐ Chick Webb   ☐ Louis Maliou Jones

☐ Aaron Douglas   ☐ Jacob Lawrence

1. an African-American painter, illustrator, and arts educator

2. an African-American painter known for his portrayal of African-American life

3. an American jazz musician and singer-songwriter with a career spanning nearly thirty years

4. an American jazz and swing music drummer as well as a band leader

5. an artist who painted and influenced others during the Harlem Renaissance and beyond, during her long teaching and artistic career

18. Match the art form with the country.

☐ Japan   1. Aztec headress

☐ China   2. Wall quilt

☐ Mexico   3. Kimono

☐ India   4. Cut paper

19. Match the stock market terms with their definition.

☐ Broker

☐ Bull Market

☐ Exchange

☐ Index

☐ Bear Market

1. The stock market being in a down trend

2. A prolonged period of increasing stock prices

3. A person who buys or sells an investment for you in exchange for a fee

4. A place in which different investments are traded

5. A benchmark which is used as a reference marker for traders and portfolio managers

20. Match the food with the country.

☐ Tabbouleh

☐ Tiki Masala

☐ Gazpacho

☐ Pad Thai

☐ Escargo

1. Thailand

2. Spain

3. France

4. India

5. Lebanon

Notes

_____
_____
_____
_____
_____
_____
_____
_____
_____

1. Circle the five elements that the Greeks taught.

Earth   Plutonium

Oxygen   Fire

Water   Radon

Carbon   Ether

Air   Silver

2. Alchemy is ☐

a. the branch of science that deals with the identification of the substances of which matter is composed

b. the medieval forerunner of chemistry, based on the supposed transformation of matter

c. natural science, especially physical science

3. Label the parts of the periodic table.

☐ Atomic Weight

☐ Element State

☐ Atomic Number

☐ Name of Element

☐ Chemical Symbol

Xenon —— 5
*** —— 4
Xe — 3
— 2
131.29   54 — 1

4. Label the parts of the atom

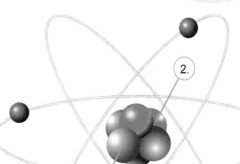

2.

3.

4.

1.

Proton
Electron
Nucleus
Neutron

1.

2.

3.

4.

Science

5. Fill in the missing information in this chemical equation:

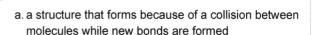

_____ HgO = _____ Hg + _____ O_2

6. Ionic bonds are formed by

a. exchanging electrons

b. gluing together

c. sharing electrons

7. Match the type of chemical bond with its description.

☐ Polar bond

☐ Ionic bond

☐ Hydrogen bond

☐ Covalent bond

1. A chemical bond formed between two ions with opposite charges

2. Also called a molecular bond; a chemical bond that involves the sharing of electron pairs between atoms

3. A covalent bond between two atoms where the electrons forming the bond are unequally distributed

4. A weak bond between two molecules resulting from an electrostatic attraction between a proton in one molecule and an electronegative atom in the other

8. A catalyst is ☐

a. a structure that forms because of a collision between molecules while new bonds are formed

b. a substance that accepts a proton and has a high pH

c. a substance that increases the rate of a chemical reaction without itself undergoing any permanent chemical change

9. Mitosis is ☐

a. The series of events that take place in a cell leading to its division and duplication.

b. a type of cell division that results in two daughter cells each having the same number and kind of chromosomes as the parent nucleus, typical of ordinary tissue growth

c. The longest phase of the cell cycle in which the cell increases in size and makes a copy of its DNA

10. Meiosis is ☐

a. The process by which organisms sexually produce sex cells (egg & sperm) through the separation of chromosomes in the nucleus of a cell into 4 chromatids and distribute those chromatids into 4 different cells

b. The process in which the cytoplasm of a single eukaryotic cell is divided to form two daughter cells following the telophase of Mitosis and Meiosis.

c. The process by which a cell makes a copy of the DNA found within the nucleus.

11. A haploid cell is ☐

a. A double rod, X-shaped structure of DNA and protein formed when the DNA condenses and duplicates

b. 1/2 of the structure of a chromosome

c. a cell that has half the usual number of chromosomes

12. A diploid cell is ☐

a. The center structure within a chromosome that joins the chromatids

b. a cell containing two complete sets of chromosomes, one from each parent

c. structures that form during the cell cycle responsible for the formation of spindle fibers

13. A mutation is ☐

a. the genetically inherited condition in which there is a marked deficiency of pigmentation in skin, hair, and eyes

b. an incorrect 19th century theory about the inheritance of characteristics

c. the changing of the structure of a gene, resulting in a variant form that may be transmitted to subsequent generations, caused by the alteration of single base units in DNA, or the deletion, insertion, or rearrangement of larger sections of genes or chromosomes

Science

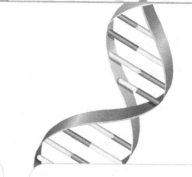

14.

Match the genetic researcher with the discovery.

☐ James Watson   ☐ Thomas Hunt Morgan

☐ Norman Borlaug   ☐ Gregor Mendel

☐ Rosalind Franklin

1. Augustinian monk and botanist whose experiments in breeding garden peas led to his eventual recognition as founder of the science of genetics

2. British X-ray crystallographer whose diffraction images, made by directing X-rays at DNA, provided crucial information that led to the discovery of its structure as a double helix

3. American molecular biologist, geneticist, and zoologist, best known as one of the co-discoverers of the structure of DNA in 1953

4. American biologist and humanitarian who led initiatives worldwide that contributed to the extensive increases in agricultural production, termed the Green Revolution

5. American evolutionary biologist, geneticist, embryologist, and science author who won the Nobel Prize in Physiology or Medicine in 1933 for discoveries elucidating the role that the chromosome plays in heredity

15. Put the DNA replication process in the correct order.

☐ Free-floating nucleotides match with each strand

☐ Two identical strands are formed.

☐ Two strands separate

16. A chromosome is ☐

a. A threadlike structure of nucleic acids and protein found in the nucleus of most living cells, carrying genetic information in the form of genes

b. A large organic molecule that stores the genetic code for the synthesis of proteins

c. An individual who is heterozygous for a trait that only shows up in the phenotype of those who are homozygous recessive

17. Weather is ___, while climate is ___.

1. the state of the atmosphere at a place and time as regards heat, dryness, sunshine, wind, rain, etc.

2. the weather conditions prevailing in an area in general or over a long period

3. the branch of science concerned with the processes and phenomena of the atmosphere, especially as a means of forecasting the weather

a. 1 and 3

b. 2 and 3

c. 1 and 2

18. The Coriolis effect

a. an effect whereby a mass moving in a rotating system experiences a force acting perpendicular to the direction of motion and to the axis of rotation

b. a system of winds rotating inward to an area of low atmospheric pressure, with a counterclockwise or clockwise circulation

c. a storm with a violent wind, in particular a tropical cyclone in the Caribbean

19. Match the type of weather front.

☐ occluded front ☐ cold front

☐ warm front ☐ stationary front

1. the boundary of an advancing mass of cold air, in particular the trailing edge of the warm sector of a low-pressure system

2. the boundary of an advancing mass of warm air, in particular the leading edge of the warm sector of a low-pressure system

3. a composite front produced by occlusion

4. a pair of air masses, neither of which is strong enough to replace the other

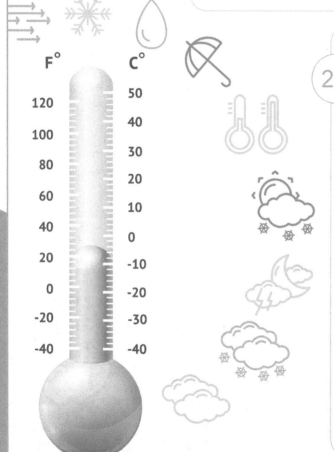

20. Match the type of storm.

☐ typhoon ☐ thunderstorm

☐ tornado ☐ hurricane

1. a storm with thunder and lightning and also typically heavy rain or hail

2. a mobile, destructive vortex of violently rotating winds having the appearance of a funnel-shaped cloud and advancing beneath a large storm system

3. a tropical storm in the region of the Indian or western Pacific oceans

4. a storm with a violent wind, in particular a tropical cyclone in the Caribbean

1. Match the prophet with his work or message.

Isaiah	Confronted David about his sin
Jeremiah	Calls Israel to repent and rebuild the temple
Ezekiel	Saw a vision of dry bones being made alive
Daniel	Was also a priest
Jonah	Was sent to Nineveh
Obadiah	Prophesied about the Messiah
Haggai	Was a prophet in Babylon
Samuel	Anointed Israel's first king
Nathan	Preached about God's justice

2. Put the events of Joseph's life in order.

_____ Became a ruler in Egypt

_____ Sold as a slave

_____ Given a coat of many colors

_____ Reunited with his brothers

_____ Made friends with a baker

_____ Thrown into a pit

_____ Worked for Potipher

_____ Interpreted Pharoah's dream

_____ Became a Father

_____ Sent to prison

3. Match the event of Jesus' ministry with the description.

1. Jesus turned water into wine
2. Jesus caused the blind to see
3. Jesus appeared to His disciples
4. Jesus resurrected the dead
5. Jesus healed someone of bleeding

☐ Road to Emmaus

☐ Mary and Martha's Home

☐ Healing of Bartemaus

☐ Journey to Jairus' House

☐ Wedding at Cana

4. Esther was

5. A concordance is used for

6. Circle the uses of a Bible dictionary.

See pictures of Bible objects

Learn Greek words

Learn about customs in Bible times

Learn Hebrew words

Learn definitions of words

Find verses about a topic

7. Look up these passages:

Proverbs 12:1

Galatians 3:22

Joshua 24:14

8. Find these locations on the map below.

Egypt   Ur of Chaldea

Euphrates River   Tigris River

Mt. Ararat   Babylon

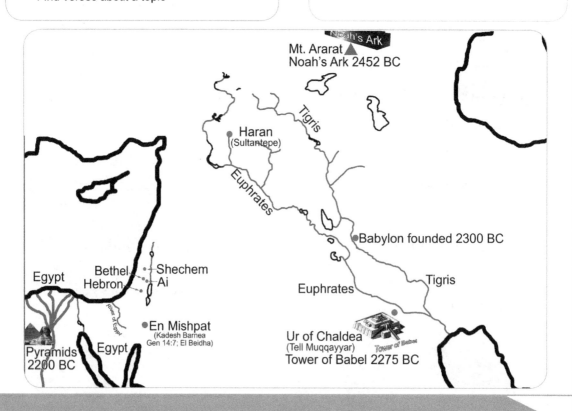

Bible

9. Fill in the blanks for Eph. 4:29 (NIV).

Do not let any _____ talk come out of your mouths, but only

what is _____ for _____ others up according to

their _____, that it may _____ those who listen.

10. Fill in the blanks for Psalm 1 (NIV).

_____ is the one who does not _____ in step with the wicked

or _____ in the way that sinners take or _____ in the company of

mockers, but whose delight is in the _____ of the Lord, and who meditates on

his law day and _____.

11. Put these verses of the Roman Road in order.

_____ Romans 3:23

_____ Romans 5:8

_____ Romans 10:13

_____ Romans 6:23

_____ Romans 10:9-10

_____ Romans 10:23

12. Fill in the blanks for John 1:9-10 (NIV).

If we _____ our sins, he is faith-

ful and just and will _____ us our

sins and purify us from all _____.

If we claim we have not sinned, we make

him out to be a _____ and his

_____ is not in us.

13. Atonement means

a. the action or process of forgiving or being forgiven

b. the reconciliation of God and humankind through Jesus Christ

c. sincere regret or remorse

37

Bible

14. Circle the examples of repentance.

Saying mean things   Insisting on my own way

Obeying parents   Looking out for others

Saying kind things   Disobeying parents

15. A covenant is

a. a declaration or assurance that one will do a particular thing or that a particular thing will happen

b. the reconciliation of God and human-kind through Jesus Christ

c. an agreement between two or more persons

16. Redemption is

a. the action of saving or being saved from sin, error, or evil

b. the action or process of forgiving or being forgiven

c. a declaration or assurance that one will do a particular thing or that a particular thing will happen declaration or assurance that one will do a particular thing or that a particular thing will happen

17. George Müller was known for

18. George Whitefield was known for

19. William Carey was a missionary to

20. Amy Carmichael was known for

STUDENT PLACEMENT TEST ADMINISTRATOR GUIDE

In the following pages, you will find the student placement test administrator guide. This section walks you through assessing your child during the test and includes an answer key and scoring chart.

SECTIONS

Each subject test is divided into 5 sections. This allows you to break up the test as needed and evaluate based on both individual section scores and an overall subject score.

ASSESS

This column includes questions and information to help you understand the goal of the test question. Use these questions to help identify and assess knowledge of the subject matter or understanding of processes, whether or not your child answers correctly.

ANSWERS

This column indicates the correct answer for the questions. Occasionally this column is merged with the notes column to give ample room for detailed answer information.

NOTES

In order to help you understand how a child should arrive at an answer, we have included this section to give the details of the processes. As well, this area includes helpful tips on the goals for the question and how your child should arrive at answers.

✓ SCORES

Use this area to indicate a correct answer or sufficient knowledge to give credit for the question. Use either a checkmark or a number one. As your child completes each section, add up the marks and place the total in the "Section Score" box at the top of the section. These scores will be used to tally your child's subject and overall scores at the end of the test.

SUMMARY

The final page of this section is used to summarize the section scores, subject scores, and overall grade placement.

TEST HACKS

Combat test nervousness and reduce stress by utilizing some of these Test Hacks.

1. Prepare snacks in advance, including protein to munch on during the test and other snacks for break time.

2. When choosing a test location, consider where your child learns best, even if that means lounging in a hammock or sitting on an exercise ball.

3. Grab a stress ball, Silly Putty, gum, or other little tools to have on hand to combat fidgetiness.

4. If your child seems nervous, add in a little fun by periodically surprising them with a question like, "What is your favorite color?" or asking them to do something funny like draw a goofy alien with horns.

5. If you begin seeing signs of stress during the test, take a break to do jumping jacks, take 10 deep breaths, or go for a 15-minute walk or bike ride.

6. Diffusing a citrus oil like lemon, grapefruit, or orange is good to alleviate stress and improve focus without using overly calming scents like lavender.

PLACEMENT TEST GUIDE

Use when administering and scoring

STUDENT PLACEMENT TEST GUIDE

#	Assess	Answer	Solution	✔
COORDINATE PLANE			Section Score	
1	Does your child know what a coordinate plane is?	graph on page 42	Find the first number in the set on the X plane. Now move up or down to find the second number of on the Y plane. Where those two lines meet, draw a dot.	
2	Does your child know how to identify plots?	1: 2,2 3: -2,1 2: -3,0 4: 3,-1		
3	Does your child understand how to use the	4		
4	X and Y axes?	3		
PROPORTIONS AND GEOMETRIC PROPORTIONS			Section Score	
5	Does your child understand proportions?	number of cupcakes: 1,2,3,4,5,6,7,8 tablespoons of icing: 4,8,12,16,20,24,28,32		
6	Does your child know how to make tables and graphs?	graph on page 42		
7	Does your child understand percentages?	3	Note that the rectangle size is being reduced by 33%; not to be confused with finding 33% of the original rectangle size (which would be answer 2).	
8	Does your child know how to make and compare geometric shapes?	A = 2 sq. in.	$A = (b \times h) \div 2$ $A = (4 \times 1) \div 2$ $A = 4 \div 2$ $A = 2$ sq. in.	
GEOMETRY			Section Score	
9	Does your child know the formula for the area of the square.	A = 9 sq. in.	First, find the length of the sides. $P = 4S$ $12 = 4S$ $12 \div 4 = S \div 4$ $3 = S$ Now find the area. $A = S^2$ $A = 3^2$ $A = 9$ sq. in.	
10	Does your child understand symmetry and how to construct triangles?	Draw a 2 in. horizontal line. Find the middle of the line and follow it up to any height. Draw a dot. Now connect the dot to either side of the triangle.		
11	Does your child know the formula for the volume of a pyramid?	V = 12 m³	$V = (l \times w \times h) \div 3$ $V = (3 \times 3 \times 4) \div 3$ $V = 36 \div 3$ $V = 12$ m³	
12	Is your child familiar with vertical, congruent, complementary, supplementary, adjacent, corresponding, alternate interior, and alternate exterior angles?	A. Corresponding B. Adjacent C. Complementary D. Alternate Interior	E. Congruent F. Alternate Exterior G. Vertical H. Supplementary	

#	Assess	Answer	Solution	✔
ALGEBRA AND NUMBER LINE			Section Score	
13	Does your child know how to substitute a number for an unknown?	x = 25	5x = 25 x 5 5x = 125 5x ÷ 5 = 125 ÷ 5 x = 25	
14	Does your child understand the order of operations?	29	8 + [7 + (18 + 2)] - 6 8 + [7 + 20] - 6 8 + 27 - 6 35 - 6 29	
15	Can your child work with negative numbers?	-3		
16	Can your child compare numbers on a number line?	a. -69 b. 1.2 c. 1/2		
PROBABILITY AND STATISTICS			Section Score	
17	Does your child know how to calculate probability?		First, add how many pieces of fruit total, which is 15. Now, create a proportion of apples/15. 5/15 reduced to lowest terms is 1/3. The chances are 1 out of 3.	
18	Does your child know how to read graphs? Green 15% Blue 8% Hazel 42% Brown 35%		First, find the total number of students: 26 Now find what percentage of the total each eye color is: Blue = 2/26 = 1/13 = 8% Green = 4/26 = 2/13 = 15% Hazel = 11/26 = 42% Brown = 9/26 = 35% Now draw a circle. To find the size of each arc, multiply each percentage by 360 degrees Blue = 29 degrees Green = 54 degrees Hazel = 151 degrees Brown = 126 degrees Now label each section of the circle with the correct eye color.	
19	Does your child know what mean, median, range, and mode are?	Mean: 15 Median: 14 Range: 12-20 Mode: 12	Mean: add all the numbers together and divide by the number of numbers. Median: put the numbers in order and find the number that is between the two middle numbers. Range: look at the smallest number and the largest number. Mode: find the number that is repeated the most.	
20	Can your child make a bar graph?	graph on page 42		

1.

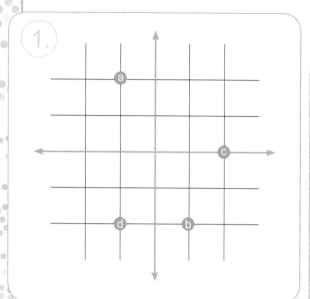

20. Create a bar graph for the following information:

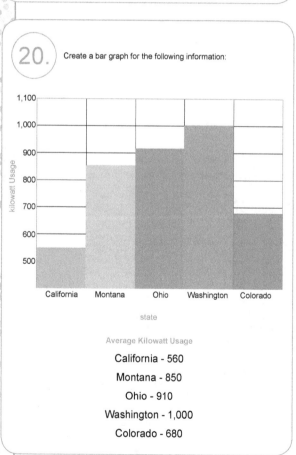

Average Kilowatt Usage

California - 560

Montana - 850

Ohio - 910

Washington - 1,000

Colorado - 680

6. Use the proportions above to fill in missing information.

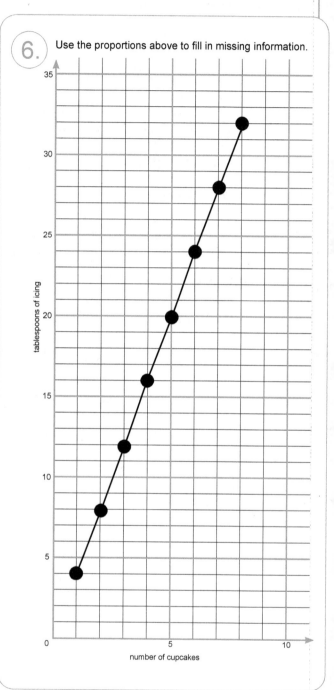

STUDENT PLACEMENT TEST GUIDE

#	Assess	Answer	✔
WRITING AND RESEARCH		Section Score	
1	Is your child familiar with book reports, summaries, descriptive essays, stories, and poems?	book report: d summary: e descriptive essay: a story: c poem: b	
2	Does your child know the basics of a research essay?	title introduction conclusion bibliography	
3	Is your child familiar with descriptive, narrative, persuasive, and compare and contrast essays?	descriptive: b narrative: a persuasive: d compare and contrast: c	
4	Is your child familiar with the writing process?	Acceptable answers may include: plan a schedule, select a topic, go over the requirements, research, draft, revise, proofread, type a final draft. Your student may still need some input, but most of the work should be done completely independently.	
SPEAKING AND LISTENING		Section Score	
5	Is your child comfortable speaking with adults?	These questions are meant to help you understand your student and help him or her become more comfortable in social situations.	
6	Is your child comfortable with social situations?		
7	Would your child be able to give a speech?	If not, look for opportunities to share with family or friends.	
8	Does your child use standard English while speaking?	raining heavily am not in trouble please be quiet obstinate	
SPELLING AND VOCABULARY		Section Score	
9	Is your child able to guess the meaning of a word by looking at the roots?	ambi: c dent: a biblio: e eu: b carnis: d	
10	Does your child know how to use a thesaurus?	a.	
11	Does your child have a wide vocabulary?	abate: 4 docile: 1 beseech: 5 exuberant: 3 canny: 2	
12	Does your child check his or her own spelling and correct it?	acheivement dispise musculer scholer occassionally	

STUDENT PLACEMENT TEST GUIDE

#	Assess	Answer	✔
GRAMMAR AND USAGE		Section Score	
13	Does your child understand what a prepositional phrase is?	to the store out of the freezer of people	
14	Does your child know how to make a verb agree with a compound subject?	were are am is	
15	Is your child familiar with direct object, indirect objects, predicate nouns, and predicate adjectives?	direct object: 3 indirect object: 4 predicate noun: 2 predicate adjective: 1	
16	Is your child familiar with participles, participial phrases, gerunds, gerund phrases, infinitives, and infinitive phrases?	participle: 3 gerund phrase: 1 participle phrase: 5 infinitive: 6 gerund: 2 infinitive phrase: 4	
LITERATURE		Section Score	
17	Is your child familiar with different types of poetry?	sonnet: 2 lyric: 4 limerick: 1 haiku: 3	
18	Does your child know what a soliloquy is?	c.	
19	Is your child familiar with point of view, internal conflict, and external conflict?	point of view: 2 internal conflict: 3 external conflict: 1	
20	Is your child familiar with irony, flashback, and foreshadowing?	irony: c flashback: b foreshadowing: a	

Notes

STUDENT PLACEMENT TEST GUIDE

#	Assess	Answer	✔
WORLD HISTORY		Section Score	
1	Is your child familiar with World War II?	Nazi Party: 4 Japanese Expansion: 1 Appeasement: 2 Treaty of Versailles: 5 Fascism: 3	
2	Is your child familiar with imperialism?	b.	
3	Is your child familiar with totalitarianism?	c.	
4	Has your child heard of the Russian Revolution?	Rasputin: b Russian Social-Democrat Labor Party: a Communist Party: e Nicholas II: c Vladimir Lenin: d	
WORLD GEOGRAPHY		Section Score	
5	Does your child know basic physical features from around the world?	Caucasus Mountains: 4 Lake Ladoga: 2 Volga River: 1 Mediterranean Sea: 3 The Alps: 5	
6	Does your child know the location of major European countries?	Russia: 4 Spain: 2 Ukraine: 5 Sweden: 1 France: 3	
7	Does your child know the capitals of major European countries?	Germany - Berlin Italy - Rome Turkey - Istanbul Poland - Warsaw UK - London	
8	Does your child know the languages of major European countries?	German - Germany French - France Italian - Italy Polish - Poland English - UK	
UNITED STATES HISTORY		Section Score	
9	Is your child familiar with the Spanish-American War?	Battle of Santiago: 3 Treaty of Paris: 4 Emilio Auginaldo: 5 USS Maine: 1 William McKinley: 2	
10	Does your child know anything about the Roaring Twenties?	Yankee Stadium: 3 Palmer Raids: 1 Kellogg–Briand Pact: 5 Earnest Hemingway: 4 Warren G. Harding: 2	
11	Is your child familiar with the Great Depression?	Construction boom ends Stock market crashes Economic excess Bank panics	
12	Does your child know anything about World War II?	Lend-Lease Act Invasion of North Africa Liberation of the Philippines	

#	Assess	Answer	✓
UNITED STATES GEOGRAPHY		Section Score	
13	Can your child name some of the physical features of the United States?	Rocky Mountains: 4 Denali: 3 Mississippi River: 1 Lake Superior: 2 Gulf of Mexico: 5	
14	Can your child name the states and capitals?	Nebraska: 2 Austin: 4 Oregon: 1 Richmond: 5 New Mexico: 3	
15	Does your child have an idea of the sizes of cities in the United States?	Chicago: 3 Philadelphia: 5 Houston: 4 Los Angeles: 2 New York: 1	
16	Is your child familiar with different regions of the United State?	Sun Belt: 3 West Coast: 1 Mason-Dixon Line: 2	
CULTURES		Section Score	
17	Is your child familiar with the Harlem Renaissance?	Billie Holiday: 3 Chick Webb: 4 Aaron Douglas: 1 Louis Maliou Jones: 5 Jacob Lawrence: 2	
18	Does your child appreciate art from different places and times?	Japan: 3 China: 4 Mexico: 1 India: 2	
19	Does your child know what the stock market is?	Broker : 3 Bull Market: 2 Exchange: 4 Index: 5 Bear Market:1	
20	Does your child appreciate international cuisine?	Tabbouleh: 5 Tiki Masala: 4 Gazpacho: 2 Pad Thai: 1 Escargo: 3	

Notes

STUDENT PLACEMENT TEST GUIDE

#	Assess	Answer	✓
ATOMIC STRUCTURE		Section Score	
1	Does your child know how elements were described at different times in history?	Earth Water Air Fire Ether	
2	Is your child familiar with alchemy?	b.	
3	Does your child know how to use a periodic table?	Atomic Weight: 2 Element State: 4 Atomic Number: 1 Name of Element: 5 Chemical Symbol: 3	
4	Does your child know the parts of an atom?	1. Electron 2. Proton 3. Neutron 4. Nucleus	
CHEMICAL BONDS AND REACTIONS		Section Score	
5	Can your child balance a chemical equation?	$2\ HgO = 2\ Hg + 1\ O_2$	
6	Is your child aware that atoms exchange electrons?	a.	
7	Is your child familiar with different types of chemical bonds?	Polar bond: 3 Ionic bond: 1 Hydrogen bond: 4 Covalent bond: 2	
8	Does your child know what a catalyst is?	c.	
CELL DIVISION		Section Score	
9	Is your child familiar with mitosis?	b.	
10	Is your child familiar with meiosis?	a.	
11	Does your child know what a haploid cell is?	c.	
12	Does your child know what a diploid cells is?	b.	

#	Assess	Answer	✓
GENETICS		Section Score	
13	Does your child understand what a mutation is?	c.	
14	Is your child familiar with well-known scientists?	James Watson: 3 Norman Borlaug: 4 Rosalind Franklin: 2 Thomas Hunt Morgan: 5 Gregor Mendel: 1	
15	Is your child familiar with how DNA replicates?	1. Two strands separate 2. Free-floating nucleotides match with each strand 3. Two identical strands are formed.	
16	Can your child describe a chromosome?	a.	
WEATHER		Section Score	
17	Does your child know the difference between weather and climate?	c.	
18	Can your child describe the Coriolis effect?	a.	
19	Is your child familiar with weather fronts?	occluded front: 3 warm front: 2 cold front: 1 stationary front: 4	
20	Can your child describe different types of storms?	typhoon: 3 tornado: 2 thunderstorm: 1 hurricane: 4	

Notes

STUDENT PLACEMENT TEST GUIDE

#	Assess	Answer	✔
BIBLE STORIES		Section Score	
1	Does your child understand that prophets called God's people to repentance and pointed forward to Christ?	Isaiah - prophesied about the Messiah Jeremiah - was also a priest Ezekiel - saw a vision of dry bones being made alive Daniel - was a prophet in Babylon Jonah - was sent to Nineveh Obadiah - preached about God's justice Haggai - called Israel to repent and rebuild the temple Samuel - anointed Israel's first king Nathan - confronted David about his sin	
2	Is your child aware that Joseph was a son of Jacob?	1. Given a coat of many colors 2. Thrown into a pit 3. Sold as a slave 4. Worked for Potipher 5. Sent to prison 6. Made friends with a baker 7. Interpreted Pharoah's dream 8. Became a ruler in Egypt 9. Became a father 10. Reunited with his brothers	
3	Does your child understand the significance of Jesus' signs and wonders?	Road to Emmaus - 3. Jesus appeared to His disciples Mary and Martha's Home - 4. Jesus resurrected the dead Healing of Bartemaus - 2. Jesus caused the blind to see Journey to Jairus' House - 5. healed someone of bleeding Wedding at Cana - 1. Jesus turned water into wine	
4	Does your child understand that God uses people to accomplish His will?	Acceptable answers include: a Jew, the wife of Ahasuerus, the one who saved her people, Mordecai's niece, a queen	
BIBLE REFERENCE TOOLS		Section Score	
5	Does your child understand that a concordance can help him or her find a particular passage?	Acceptable answers include: finding verses about a topic, learning Greek words, learning Hebrew words, getting meanings of specific words in the Bible	
6	Does your child know that he or she can use a Bible dictionary to look up words he or she does not understand?	See pictures of Bible objects Learn about customs in Bible times Learn definitions of words	
7	Is your child able to find all passages quickly without using the table of contents or singing a song?	This is a subjective question. Just watch to see that your child goes to the correct testament, book, chapter, then verse without using the table of contents.	

#	Assess	Answer	✔
8	Does your child understand that the places in the Bible really existed?	See that your student is pointing to the correct locations.	

BIBLE PASSAGES		Section Score	
9	Does your child know that he or she should guard his or her words?	unwholesome; helpful; building; needs; benefit	
10	Does your child understand the difference between a righteous man and a wicked man?	Blessed; walk; stand; sit; law; night	
11	Can your child explain the way of salvation?	Romans 3:23 Romans 6:23 Romans 5:8 Romans 10:9-10 Romans 10:13 Romans 10:23	
12	Does your child understand that Jesus is the light and that we are to walk in the light?	confess; forgive; unrighteousness; liar; word	

THEOLOGY		Section Score	
13	Does your child understand that a perfect blood sacrifice was needed for sin and that all sacrifices in the Old Testament pointed to Christ?	b.	
14	Does your child know that repentance involves ceasing to do wrong and beginning to do right?	Obeying parents Saying kind things Looking out for others	
15	Can your child explain that a covenant is an agreement between two or more persons?	c.	
16	Does your child understand that believers are bought with the blood of Christ?	a.	

CHURCH HISTORY AND MISSIONS		Section Score	
17	Is your child familiar with the names of missionaries?	Acceptable answers include: his work with orphans, his belief that he should not trust in a bank account, his prayer life, his wild youth	
18	Does your child take an interest in other countries and cultures?	Acceptable answers include: his sermons, the Great Awakening, his booming voice	
19	Does your child desire to meet the needs of others?	India	
20		Acceptable answers include: her work with young girls, her work in India, her brown eyes, her disguises	

MATH

Score	Section
	Coordinate Plane
	Proportions & Geometric Proportions
	Geometry
	Algebra & Number Line
	Probability & Statistics

Total Score

Grade Placement

LANGUAGE ARTS

Score	Section
	Writing & Research
	Speaking & Listening
	Spelling & Vocabulary
	Grammar & Usage
	Literature

Total Score

Grade Placement

HISTORY & GEOGRAPHY

Score	Section
	World History
	World Geography
	United States History
	United States Geography
	Culture

Total Score

Grade Placement

SCIENCE

Score	Section
	Atomic Structure
	Chemical Bonds & Reactions
	Cell Division
	Genetics
	Weather

Total Score

Grade Placement

BIBLE

Score	Section
	Bible Stories
	Bible Reference Tools
	Bible Passages
	Theology
	Church History & Missions

Total Score

Grade Placement

STUDENT PLACEMENT SCORING

The Well Planned Start was designed to assess a grade level *per subject.* Use the key below to *determine the grade level for each subject.*

1. Each correct answer is valued at 1 point. Count the number in each section. Write the number in the score box to the left of the section.

2. Add the section scores together and place the total in the **Total Score** box.

3. Using the key below, determine the grade assessment for *each subject.*

SUBJECT TEST KEY

- Total Score = 20: Administer the 8th grade test for this subject. Your child may be ready for 9th grade.
- Total Score = 15-19: Your child is ready for the 7th grade.
- Total Score = 10-14: Base your decision on the following **section scores.**
  - Score 2 or less in 1-2 sections: Your child is ready for the 8th grade in this subject, but you can expect to give extra help throughout the year.
  - Score 2 or less in 3-5 sections: Your child should begin this subject at a 7th grade level.
- All sections = 0-9: Administer the 6th grade test for this subject. Your child needs additional evaluation.

BIBLE EXCEPTION

Because the development of spiritual growth is not confined to a grade level, the Bible tests for Well Planned Start were designed to cover a range through the following stages of education:

- Starting Out - Preschool - 1st Grade
- Getting Exciting: 2nd - 4th Grade
- Beginning to Understand: 5th - 8th Grade
- Learning to Reason: 9th - 12th Grade

When scoring Bible and determining placement, it is recommended to use your discretion in deciding if additional testing is needed or more time studying the topics covered.

WHAT NEXT?

Compare your findings to the parent assessment test and begin to make a plan of action on the following page.

If you suspect a learning challenge or special needs, we strongly recommend additional testing with a specialist.

MATH

grade

_____

_____

_____

_____

_____

_____

_____

LANGUAGE ARTS

grade

_____

_____

_____

_____

_____

_____

_____

HISTORY & GEOGRAPHY

grade

_____

_____

_____

_____

_____

_____

_____

SCIENCE

_____
_____
_____
_____
_____
_____

BIBLE

_____
_____
_____
_____
_____
_____

PLAN OF ACTION

Your child has completed the test, the scores are tallied, and a grade level is determined. But, it doesn't stop there! Here are some ways to utilize the information gleaned from this assessment to help you and your child tackle the new school year with confidence!

HOMESCHOOL

Use this space to note your child's grade level, gaps you observed during testing, areas where your child excels, and specific strategies you will be seeking as you choose curriculum. Make a list of academic needs for the coming year, and have that list on hand to check against the content in your curricula of choice.

HYBRIDS - CO-OP, TUTORIAL, & ENRICHMENTS

If your child is involved in homeschool classes taught through a co-op, use this area to note learning needs to discuss with your child's teacher(s). Also, make note of any enrichment activities you can do with your child to fill in gaps and strengthen weaknesses.

TRADITIONAL SCHOOL

If your child attends a private or public school, make note of areas you want to discuss with your child's teacher(s) to determine how to strengthen weaknesses. At home, plan trips or organize evening discussion to cater to strengths and incorporate Bible training.

BEGINNING TO UNDERSTAND

7th grade

PARENT TEACHING TIPS

Somewhere around fourth or fifth grade, a tangible change begins to take place in your child. Connections start clicking into place. Light bulbs come on. An understanding dawns. The change is subtle at first, but, as you ask comprehension questions, discuss prayer requests, or explore the impact of experiences, you will notice a new depth to your child's conversational contributions.

These understanding years, typically fitting into what is now referred to as middle school, form a bridge between the years of excitement and the deeper thinking required in high school.

So, what does this look like practically?

1. Do the algebra. Many of you are groaning right now, but algebraic equations are a perfect example of the connections being made during this stage. Children will begin to learn that if A+B=C and D+E=C, then it must follow that A+B=D+E. The connections occur as often in everyday life as they do in math, science, and logic. Learning the dreaded algebraic formulas truly does help growing minds process the connection and balance in other areas.

2. Explore inferences. A paragraph that discusses "steam rising from wet pavement as the clouds parted, allowing the hot summer sun to beat down unhindered" might indicate a summer storm has just blown through. The storm itself is not clearly described, but one can make inferences from the information given. Exploring inferences not only helps children improve their reading comprehension, it also helps them explore clues around them in life.

3. Pull the tidbits together. In previous years, your child learned facts about the American and French revolutions. Now it is time to show how events happening on one side of the Atlantic Ocean actually connected to and even impacted events occurring on the opposite side. This is true not only across history, but also in the ways science, history, mathematics, and life in general have coincided through the centuries.

4. The key to this stage is teaching your child how to look beyond facts and learn to make connections, seeing how those facts relate.

In the following pages you will find practical teaching tips and activity suggestions for every concept covered in the placement test. Here are some ways to utilize these tips:

1. Use the suggested activities to strengthen low-scoring areas.

2. For strong areas, focus on activities that will keep your child challenged.

3. At times, having a negative experience with academics can take the joy out of learning. Restore that joy gently by choosing activities that will be fun for your child.

4. Use enrichment activities to put together a "summer camp." This is the perfect time to fill in gaps and bring kids up to grade level.

5. If you are homeschooling, utilize some of these activities on days that are too interrupted or chaotic for the normal school schedule. You can also use them for a relaxed "Friday Fun Day!"

6. Liven up a co-op class by incorporating some of these activities.

PARENT TEACHING TIPS

To use throughout the entire year!

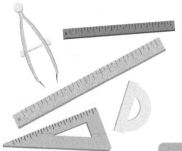

Math

THE COORDINATE PLANE

- Create a practice grid on a whiteboard marker. Use a Sharpie to make the grid and dry-erase markers for practice.

- Print worksheets or get a workbook for extra practice.

- Plot out coordinates that create a picture, then have your child figure out the picture.

- Check your child's work promptly.

PROPORTIONS AND GEOMETRIC PROPORTIONS

- Use equivalence tables to help your child visualize proportions.

- Invite your child write story problems for the family to solve.

- Have your child figure sales tax for percentage practice.

- Encourage your child to teach concepts back to you so you can know that she understands what she has been taught.

- Find fun ways to graph real life information.

GEOMETRY

- Have your child measure angles around your house and tell what kind of angles they are.

- Practice determining perimeter, area, and volume by measuring items around the house.

- Build something together that requires measuring angles.

- Look for parallel, perpendicular, and intersecting lines while on a nature walk.

WHOLE NUMBERS, FRACTIONS, AND DECIMALS

- Build something together.

- Bake some treats for the neighbors and practice fractions by doubling or tripling the batch.

- Learn how to sew.

- Make a fractions and decimals Bingo game. Put fractions on one side of the card and decimals on the other side. Call out a fraction or decimal, and your student must convert it to the other before marking it.

PROBABILITY AND STATISTICS

- Choose a number between 2 and 12. Now calculate the odds of rolling that number with two dice.

- Take a deck of cards and calculate the odds of drawing a cards of different values or suits.

- Flip a coin and calculate the probability a of getting heads a certain number of times in a row.

- Take the numbers of boys and girls in a family and calculate the probability of having those numbers.

JOURNAL YOUR EFFORTS

If you feel that your child is extremely behind, consider formal testing for a learning difficulty such as dyscalculia.

Language Arts

JOURNAL YOUR EFFORTS

WRITING & RESEARCH

- Enter an essay contest.
- Write an article for a church or co-op newsletter.
- Help your child research a topic of his choice and let him write a research report.
- Allow your child to read before lights out.
- Begin building your child's personal library by giving a book for each birthday and Christmas.

SPEAKING & LISTENING

- Have your child interview someone who was alive during one of the historical events you have studied.
- Find a reading list and require your student to read some of the titles.
- Watch a movie based on a book.
- Enjoy read aloud time as a family and take turns reading.
- Let your child check out any books that interest him or her.

GRAMMAR & USAGE

- Practice diagramming sentences.
- Take turns looking up words in the thesaurus and reading the synonyms.
- Find a penpal for your child.
- Let your child try writing a novel.
- Write thank you notes.

LITERATURE

- Take turns reading aloud.
- Discuss what your child is reading.
- Host a poetry recitation party.
- Provide a checklist for your child to revise his or her own work.
- Show your child how to make an outline of his or her writing.
- If you feel that your child is extremely behind, consider formal testing for a learning difficulty such as dyslexia or dysgraphia.

SPELLING & VOCABULARY

- Join a book club.
- Subscribe to a magazine.
- Ask the reference librarian to show your child how to use library and online resources.
- Get a word board game and have a family game night.
- Provide a notebook or journal for your student to write in.

If you feel that your child is extremely behind, consider formal testing for a learning difficulty such as dyslexia or dysgraphia.

JOURNAL YOUR EFFORTS

UNITED STATES GEOGRAPHY

- Let your child plan the next road trip.
- Shop the international aisle at the grocery store.
- Make a map of your town.
- Get involved in orienteering.
- Collect coins or stamps.

UNITED STATES HISTORY

- Immerse yourself in the art, music, and literature of an era of your choice.
- Visit local historical sites.
- Plan your next vacation around museums or historical sites.
- Explain to your child why you celebrate certain holidays.
- Make a timeline.

WORLD HISTORY

- Tell family stories.
- Go to a museum.
- Create a family scrapbook.
- Research the countries your ancestors came from.
- Make a family tree.

WORLD GEOGRAPHY

- Look at a physical map and talk about geography affects people groups.
- Get an atlas and a globe. When new place is read about, find it.
- Get a subscription to a history or geography magazine.
- Make a collage of another country.
- Get some geography games and hold a family game night.

CULTURE

- Write an editorial letter about a social issue.
- Follow the stock market for one month.
- Have a family debate about a social issue.
- Let your child choose a historical figure and research him or her.
- Read important American documents together.

Science

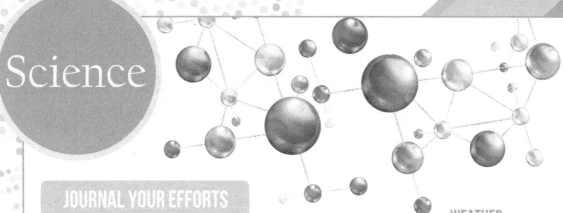

JOURNAL YOUR EFFORTS

ATOMIC STRUCTURE

- Find a puzzle or game utilizing the periodic table.

- Make atoms using paper plates and various sized candies. Form bonds between the candy atoms.

- Solve simple chemical equations together.

- When your child asks a question, research the answer together.

CHEMICAL BONDS AND REACTIONS

- Build a model of a molecule.

- Get some pH test strips and identify acids and bases around the house.

- Get a soil test kit to test some garden or potted soil. Now use the information to make the soil more fertile.

- Provide a sketchbook and colored pencils for nature observation.

- Visit the zoo or nature center.

WEATHER

- Track world weather patterns.

- Track local weather, comparing the forecast to what really happens.

- Interview a storm chaser or meteorologist.

- Learn about the different types of clouds and what they indicate.

- Learn about planes that fly into hurricanes for research purposes.

CELL DIVISION

- Make a trip to a science museum.

- Invest in a microscope and find prepared slides that show cell division.

- Follow the growth of a baby from conception to birth.

- Set aside a shelf for science and nature displays.

GENETICS

- Make a pedigree chart for some family characteristics.

- Get a pet.

- Build a DNA model.

- If finances allow, find out your heritage with a DNA kit.

- Find some science documentaries on at the library.

REFERENCE TOOLS

- Invest in a good Bible dictionary with lots of pictures.

- Choose a word or topic and help your child list all the verses about it.

- Look at biblical maps and then find the modern day locations.

- Practice Bible drills.

THEOLOGY

- Talk about how the blood of a perfect sacrifice was required for the forgiveness of sins.

- Give examples of repentance. Share how God has convicted you.

- Tell your child that only God can keep a covenant perfectly.

- Explain that believers have been purchased out of slavery to sin so that they can become slaves of Christ.

BIBLE STORIES

- Create a Bible timeline.

- Write some biographical sketches of different Bible characters.

- Find a parallel of the Gospels and read it in chronological order.

- Find information about what was happening at the same time in other areas of the world.

BIBLE PASSAGES

- Read the same passages over and over.

- Mark key words in passages.

- Practice outlining Bible passages.

- Encourage your child to take notes while listening to sermons.

CHURCH HISTORY & MISSIONS

- Read missionary biographies.

- When you study a new country, research missionaries that have served or are currently serving there.

- Get your child involved with a local or foreign missions project.

- Pray for and financially support your church's missionaries.

Bible

JOURNAL YOUR EFFORTS

MILESTONES
WHAT TO EXPECT

USING MILESTONES

The timely development of a child is a frequent question and concern among both new and experienced parents. In the following pages you will discover the physical, emotional, and academic development you can expect from your child **by the end of 7th grade**.

The goal of the Well Planned Gal milestones is to have the information on hand as a guideline. These ranges of development can greatly aid you as you parent, teach, and train your child to the next level.

It is important, however, that you do not use these milestones to "diagnose" your child as behind or gifted. It is perfectly normal for children to display a broad range of abilities as they grow and develop.

Many things may influence a child's growth and development, including temporary stress, nutrition, illness, sleep habits, premature birth, learning styles, and physical growth spurts. If you have specific concerns or questions concerning your child's physical or academic progress, we urge you to consult your child's pediatrician.

The Well Planned Gal milestones are outlined in three ranges of growth and maturity.

YOUR CHILD SHOULD BE ABLE TO . . .

This area presents what **most** children this age are comfortable doing. Approximately 80% of children fall into this category.

YOUR CHILD MAY BE ABLE TO . . .

This area presents what **many** children this age are comfortable doing. Approximately 50% of children fall into this category.

YOUR CHILD MAY EVEN TRY TO . . .

This area presents what **some** children this age attempt. Approximately 20% of children -- including gifted or exceptional children -- fall into this category.

Welcome to the wild and crazy middle school years! Not quite a teen, not really a child, your young person is thrust into an exciting time of growth and change. The Beginning to Understand stage usually covers 5th through 8th grade for children ranging in age from 9 to 14. So, as you can imagine, a great deal happens during these years! You can see why it is important, as in every stage, to consider any list of milestones to be a general guideline and not a set of hard, fast rules.

Your child's physical and emotional maturation may happen suddenly in the early years of this stage, or it may slowly dawn over a few years. Some children grow and change steadily while others grow in spurts and then hit plateaus for a while. Regardless, you will likely wake up one day and wonder who the new kid in the house is! Your middle schooler likely feels the same way, one day acting immature and the next trying to be an adult. With patience, knowledge, and love, you both can grow through this transition with a stronger relationship than ever.

As you process through this stage with your child, remember that, although high school is the next step, you have several years to work through these milestones. Beware of comparing him to others, and instead help him identify his unique talents and abilities as you also help him lay a foundation of maturity for the coming stage.

7TH GRADE MILESTONES

Understanding your child's growth

HOW YOUR CHILD IS GROWING

Date	✓	Milestone	Journal
Your child should be able to			
	☐	Go through puberty	
Your child may be able to			
	☐	Need much more sleep (10-12 hours each night)	
	☐	Eat a lot more (Growing boys and girls may eat up to four large meals a day, with frequent fruit snacks in between meals, doubling their food intake overnight.)	
Your child may even be able to			
	☐	Grow rapidly toward physical adulthood with extreme changes in height, weight, voice, facial hair, and muscles	
How you can help. You can encourage his growth through these milestones with activities like these:			
	☐	Explain bodily changes and allow them to ask questions.	
	☐	Have matter-of-fact conversations about the facts of life.	
	☐	Facilitate age-appropriate, gender-specific changes in appearance and provide needed hygiene supplies.	
	☐	Enroll in team sports or supply sports equipment for use with siblings.	
	☐	Provide a special space for personal hygiene items.	
	☐	Give your child specific household responsibilities.	
Notes			

HOW YOUR CHILD IS FEELING

Date	✓	Milestone	Journal
Your child should be able to			
	☐	Think more about the present than about the future	
	☐	Base judgments on definite concepts of right and wrong	
	☐	Desire more privacy	
	☐	Question self-worth	
	☐	Become opinionated	
	☐	Seek relationships outside of the family	
	☐	Show off	
	☐	Attempt to be more self-sufficient	
	☐	Begin to internalize family values	
	☐	Take more risks	
Your child may be able to			
	☐	Be more sensitive to what others think of him	
	☐	Adjust to the changes of puberty	
Your child may even be able to			
	☐	Desire more freedom	
	☐	Realize he is no longer a child	
	☐	Display fewer mood swings	

		How you can help. You can encourage his growth through these milestones with activities like these:	
	☐	Provide personal space and create boundaries for other members of the family.	
	☐	Give opportunity to spend time away from home.	
	☐	Affirm his value as a person.	
	☐	Allow opposing viewpoints be expressed respectfully.	
	☐	Provide opportunities to participate in deep conversation.	
	☐	Guide him in choosing good friends.	
	☐	Use advanced vocabulary.	
	☐	Encourage trying new things.	
	☐	Provide a safe place for friends to spend time.	
	☐	Model how to plan ahead.	
	☐	Share stress-control techniques.	
	☐	Assign chores and hold him accountable.	
	☐	Encourage proper behavior around members of the opposite sex.	

Notes

HOW YOUR CHILD IS LEARNING

Date	✓	Milestone	Journal
Your child should be able to			
	☐	Write a persuasive essay	
	☐	Write a business letter	
	☐	Write a research report	
	☐	Give a speech	
	☐	Study Greek and Latin roots or a modern language	
	☐	Accurately use troublesome words	
	☐	Identify lines of latitude and longitude	
	☐	Locate deserts of the world	
	☐	Add and subtract positive and negative numbers	
	☐	Solve ratio and percent problems	
	☐	Divide fractions and decimals	
	☐	Begin pre-algebra and solving problems with one variable	
	☐	Calculate speed and work	
	☐	Understand energy and force	
Your child may be able to			
	☐	Use deductive reasoning	
	☐	Argue persuasively	
	☐	Anticipate how the present impacts the future	
	☐	Distinguish fact from opinion	

	☐	Evaluate the credibility of sources	
	☐	Write an organized piece	
	☐	Understand grammatical phrases	
	☐	Identify countries and capitals of the world	
	☐	Memorize the states and capitals	
	☐	Analyze 3-D shapes	
	☐	Compare math equations	
	☐	Plot points on a coordinate plane	
	☐	Interpret data	
	☐	Understand chemical bonds	
	☐	Study genetics and explain inherited traits	
	☐	Comprehend weather patterns	

Your child may even be able to

	☐	Express deep thoughts and opinions through talking	
	☐	Participate in mature discussions	
	☐	Write in a variety of compositional styles	
	☐	Practice sentence variety	
	☐	Perform basic trigonometry	
	☐	Work with exponents	
	☐	Calculate linear data	
	☐	Understand electricity and magnetism	
	☐	Explain the behavior of light and sound	

HOW YOUR CHILD IS LEARNING

Date	✓	Milestone	Journal
	☐	Comprehend metabolism	
	☐	Study geology	
How you can help. You can encourage his growth through these milestones with activities like these:			
	☐	Assign essays and summaries.	
	☐	Read biographies together.	
	☐	Encourage journaling.	
	☐	Introduce good poetry options to analyze.	
	☐	Discuss literature.	
	☐	Assign a written report or a story.	
	☐	Provide a dictionary or use reference department of the library.	
	☐	Teach sentence diagramming.	
	☐	Listen to audio books and read aloud.	
	☐	Act out a historical event.	
	☐	Perform a play together.	
	☐	Find a debate or panel discussion to participate in.	
	☐	Teach model making.	
	☐	Provide maps for labeling.	
	☐	Visit civic buildings.	
	☐	Discuss culture, time periods, and world religion.	
	☐	Study myths together.	

CPSIA information can be obtained
at www.ICGtesting.com
Printed in the USA
LVHW061359270321
682086LV00002B/10